GENERAL CUSTER'S FINAL HOURS
Correcting A Century of Misconceived History

by
Roger Darling

Potomac-Western Press, Inc.
Vienna, Virginia

Library of Congress Catalog Card Number 91-68408

ISBN 0-9621488-2-2

First edition—February 1992
Second printing—July 1992

Books by Roger Darling

Benteen's Scout-to-the-Left: The Route from the Divide to the Morass, 1987.

Custer's Seventh Cavalry Comes To Dakota: New Discoveries Reveal Custer's Tribulations Enroute to the Yellowstone Expedition, 1988.
(The Potomac-Western Press, Inc. edition of this book won the 1988 Literary Award from the Little Big Horn Associates national organization. This edition is now out of print, and rare.)

A Sad And Terrible Blunder, Generals Terry and Custer at the Little Big Horn: New Discoveries, 1990.
(Potomac-Western Press, Inc.)
(This book won the 1990 John M. Carroll Literary Award. See page 33 for book availability.)

General Custer's Final Hours: Correcting A Century of Misconceived History, 1992. (Potomac-Western Press, Inc.)

Contents

Preface

The following treatise on General Custer's final hours by no means addresses all of the errors and historical misconceptions that have clouded public understanding of the 1876 Little Big Horn campaign for over a century. Many other aberrations are evident in the official records and extensive Custer literature.

Over the past years my books have identified and analyzed these historical inaccuracies, presenting new information discovered through extensive field research and in the historical record depositories such as the Library of Congress and National Archives in Washington, D.C.

It is encouraging that the books have been praised for enhancing historical understanding by raising significant questions challenging the conventional wisdom and traditional published accounts about Little Big Horn and Custer events. Such challenge has been made possible by the existence of that particular new information which provides new insights into Custer's character, his behavior, and his relationships both official and private. Such challenge also derives from providing something missing and long overdue in Custer literature—professional military-intelligence analysis of Custer's field tactics on June 25, 1876.

Briefly consider just a few examples where such new information has shed new light while concurrently exposing misconceived history. The heretofore unknown 1873 Terry-Custer relationship is now revealed. Its contentious origin and the subsequent personality stresses therein help explain the anomalies of their respective behavior, particularly during the 1876 expedition. Primary source material has been found that relates new dimensions of Custer's harsh leadership style, and its counterproductiveness within 7th Cavalry field operations, particularly during the Yellowstone Expedition. The true nature of the Benteen Scout, its timing, exact terrain route, the tactical and strategic purposes it actually served have been factually revealed for the first time. This important new information corrects the historical record by demonstrating the scout *was* executed in a timely and effective manner. Newly discovered letters exchanged between Benteen and Custer portray not only the peculiar circumstances and leadership tensions within their disagreeable 1873 Dakota-transfer relationship, but help explain the negative effects of such on the subsequent Yellowstone Expedition *and* 1876 campaign. The mysterious events surrounding General Terry's removal of Custer from 7th Cavalry command vice Colonel Sturgis are now known, revealing stressful crosscurrents among the officers and men that damaged regimental field operations at a critical time.

My latest book, **A Sad and Terrible Blunder, Generals Terry and Custer at the Little Big Horn: New Discoveries**, brings together and focuses attention on all this new information as it specifically relates to the 1876 campaign. It provides also that long overdue attention to Custer's field tactics, scrutinizing his actions within the framework and criteria of professional military-intelligence analysis. **Blunder** was published to help correct the historical record. It is comprehensive and seeks historical fairness. Balance is provided—criticism as well as praise are presented where deserved. In that much is commendable about Custer, Terry, Gibbon, Reno, Benteen, Sheridan, Sherman, and others such as Major Brisbin and Captain Freeman, none are seriously diminished by the warranted criticism. In fact, legitimate criticism places the character and military competence of each in more accurate historical perspective.

Yet, there is perhaps a larger purpose to be served. If praise and criticism are to be offered, *it should be for the right reasons.* For a century these men have been lauded and condemned in Custer literature, too often for the wrong reasons. The root cause of such erroneous historical judgments and evaluations is found in those 1876 campaign misconceptions.

In covering the entire campaign, the book reveals these misconceptions as they occur in the expedition's planning stages, during the field execution, and also in the battle aftermath. Each area of misunderstanding is covered in detail, casting new light on *all* campaign events. Therefore, to gain a better understanding of the *total* campaign, and thus the *complete* integrated troop-movement dynamics, (as well as those actions of the various officers deserving of either praise or criticism), it is necessary to have clear recognition of both the extent and significance of these historical inaccuracies.

In this regard, the following brief discussion of just a few selected misconceptions may be helpful. In presenting these items, two purposes are served. One is to demonstrate that while these specific misconceptions are indeed important, they represent only a portion, only a sampling of those areas of the 1876 campaign where historical inaccuracies are all too prevalent. In consequence of this, the following topics, along with many others described in **Blunder,** constitute for the reader *recommended areas of serious new study,* reexamination and reevaluation in light of the historical facts now evident.

The second purpose in presenting these selected topics is to help balance the discussion in the following treatise on Custer's final hours—to help put into proper perspective this one most prominent, highly significant, troop movement, and to analyze it in detail. This demonstrates that the various misconceptions about Custer's final maneuvers are by no means isolated phenomena unique to Custer alone, suggesting unfairly and unwarrantedly, for example, that Custer (as General Terry later claimed) was the *sole* cause of the failed Little Big Horn campaign. To the contrary, the Custer final-hours-aberrations are just part of the broader fabric of historical inaccuracies throughout the campaign, touching on the field actions of Terry, Gibbon, Reno, Benteen and the other important participants in this intriguing American historical event.

Consider the role of Colonel Gibbon's Montana troops during the early summer months of the 1876 campaign. His strategic task is invariably described as "Guarding the Yellowstone" (as one book chapter-title identifies it), ensuring that the hostile Indians did not cross north over the river and "escape" to Canada. In 1875, Generals Terry, Sheridan and Sherman, in working out the expedition's famous three-column strategy, envisaged the Montana troops under Gibbon as fully capable of this guard-duty role. Because these officers did so, subsequent writers of books, articles, and film accounts have also accepted that Montana troop role as valid and successfully carried out.

But was this strategic expectation realistic in field operational terms? Could Gibbon's men actually (and did they?) prevent Indian movement north? The answers were found in analysis of the terrain, and in scrutiny of Indian performance all around Gibbon's troops during those summer months. Such study provided fascinating insights into flawed army planning, and how it affected the 1876 campaign.

From the moment of his April arrival on the north bank of the Yellowstone River, Gibbon was unable to patrol effectively, much less defend, the enormous, broken-ground expanse where the Indians could (and did) cross at will. Gibbon's leadership proved hesitant and inept. While his scouts gathered valuable intelligence on Indian villages nearby, Gibbon did not understand its meaning or operational value.. The Indians quickly detected the obvious impotency of Gibbon's cavalry and infantry in taking offensive operations against them, and treated the Montana troops with deserved contempt. In full view the warriors hovered ominously nearby the army camp, probing selectively. Utilizing their guerrilla warfare tactics of force-dissipation, induced-uncertainty, and other techniques, the Indians intimidated, indeed humiliated, Gibbon's force all that summer.

They never crossed north to Canada. But it was not because Gibbon prevented them doing so. Indian plans were directed elsewhere. They *chose* not to cross, but had the full capability should they have so desired. Gibbon and Terry had deluded themselves into believing that Gibbon's forces actually possessed and acted with offensive capability. In reality, Gibbon was constantly on the defensive. He *never* had the field-operations initiative against the Indians.

Such misreading of Indian capability and accomplishments was pervasive in the 1876 army. It was a mental block of sorts, unfounded army presumptions of martial superiority over Indian field tactics. Such blockage had negative, self-deluding effects on officer attitudes during the subsequent June 21-25 marches of *both* Custer and the Montana troops. These planning and leadership misjudgments were not recognized at the time and notably are *still* overlooked or misunderstood in published accounts of the campaign.

Consider the details of Terry's strategic plan as it involved Custer's attack-force movements south up Rosebud Creek, *concurrent with* Gibbon's Montana troop blocking-force moving west toward the Big Horn River and Tullock Creek.

The implausibility of Terry's strategic conception is readily detectable. Terry anticipated that Custer might find the large Indian trail veering east, and cautioned Custer to watch for such a deviation even though Terry believed the Indians to be west in the Little Big Horn valley region. But by even recognizing that such a possibility existed, and that Custer would of necessity have to follow such an Indian trail east should it occur, Terry revealed himself a poor strategist. Had Custer turned east from the Rosebud, it meant that Terry had pointlessly launched Gibbon west—in the opposite direction—separating the expedition troops nearly 100 miles without joint purpose or the means of coordination, and that Custer *alone* would meet the large Indian force.

Pursuing this strategy meant that both units were weakened and thus became more vulnerable in the face of an as yet ill-defined enemy. Terry had overlooked the critical importance of keeping the troops unified *until* his target was identified, and *then* separating them into pincer columns (double-movements as Terry called them). Had Custer actually turned east, Terry's strategy would have *in 1876* been exposed as foolish and dangerous in the extreme. Overlooked then, the serious flaws and omissions in Terry's strategy have received scant attention for over a century since, writers focusing on the shallow and virtually meaningless question of whether Custer obeyed or disobeyed Terry's orders—with such a question alone suggesting unfairly that Custer was solely responsible for the plan's failure. It would have been more helpful to history for writers to demonstrate that Terry's orders did not define his *total* plan (as Terry later claimed they had); to demonstrate that Terry's plan was not legitimate (in realistic cavalry-infantry operational terms); to point out the strategic and tactical incongruities and discrepancies between Terry's plan and the incomplete or fragmentary orders given to Custer.

Consider another significant strategy-planning question. What did Terry envisage as campaign success? What acutally did he expect to accomplish? Did he believe, for example, that an initial attack would defeat the large body of Indians and turn them submissive? Would they remain in a compact, manageable body? Would the warriors (or families) allow themselves to be herded back to the Missouri River agencies? Would it be necessary to corral the warriors in some manner, disarm them for the extended march east? How would they be corralled, and what if some warriors cooperated and some did not? Did Terry have sufficient force to compel obedience relative to the vast number of Indians involved? Did Terry feel he had enough force to make a multiple effort: attack and defeat the hostile warriors, pursue them if they (some) fled, while at the same time controlling the captives? As early as June 19th, Terry learned of the sizeable Indian trail discovered on the Rosebud. Did this operational intelligence indicating a massive Indian presence make it evident he might be faced with extraordinary post-battle circumstances, and should plan for them?

Terry's strategic plan speaks to none of these questions. When at Rosebud Creek mouth, and despite three months of good campaigning weather yet remaining, Terry was in a hurry. He made no effort to mount intelligence gathering missions using his capable scout units—this to procure the operational data necessary to properly define his Indian enemy target, and on the basis of that information to design the force-structure best suited to defeat it. On June 21, Terry hastily finalized his plan and dispatched Custer after the Indians south up the Rosebud. It is known from his later writings, and from those officers who dealt personally with him at that time, that Terry fully expected the Indians to attempt to "escape" from the army. He was convinced that they would have to be fought and defeated, and then in the manner of his Civil War after-battle, mop-up operations, Terry's men would be expected to gather up the prisoners and control them. It would all be rather simple—automatically managed, so he thought.

Was Terry's strategic expectation realistic? Scrutiny of his plan (and Terry's later comments about it) reveals the shallowness of his reasoning. Terry gave no recognition to the ominous consequences of marching a divided expedition force away from the Yellowstone River to pursue this undefined, but obviously large, accumulation of Indians. He was thus unmindful that in pursuing this strategy, he risked having the entire force cut off deep in the Indian war-zone; placed under protracted siege with no army relief force within timely reach; wiped out eventually by attrition under relentless Indian attack.

These and many other important strategic contingency considerations are not covered in Custer literature. In their place has been a century of undue preoccupation with Custer alone, and of over-simplifying the military field maneuvers of the respective army forces as if each functioned in isolation. The consequences of the various troop movements *in terms of possible Indian counter-measures* are also not adequately assessed. Almost invariably the book, article, and film accounts accept as valid, and unquestionably repeat the traditional 1876 army "success theme"—i.e., the campaign troops were fully capable of locating the hostile Indians, fighting and defeating them, and bringing the conquered enemy under prompt control. Thus, not only did the army planners, and Terry himself, misconceive the strategies and field operational realities, but subsequent writers have helped to firmly cement these aberrations in Custer literature and the public consciousness.

The notion of army invincibility against the Indians was a core misconception governing the thinking of Terry and his superiors—not just in formulating strategy, but in field operations as well. The officers somehow concluded that *whatever* force-structure each army unit used, *it would prevail* against any opposing Indian forces. That this illusion was deeply rooted in Terry's thinking was proven later in the 1876 summer when he expressed what might be called a corollary to the army "success theme."

At that time, Custer and his troops were dead, and Major Reno and Captain Benteen were besieged by thousands of Indians on a blufftop near the Little Big Horn River. Unaware of these adverse conditions, Terry was marching his 400 man blocking-force of Montana troops south up the Little Big Horn valley. The Indians, who only the day before had gained superiority over the 7th Cavalry and its remnants, detected Terry's presence and quickly organized and disciplined a select warrior force. Wearing army uniforms taken from Custer's dead troopers, and maneuvering to appear as marching cavalry troop units, the Indians attempted to deceive Terry, to draw off and fragment his force, to defeat the splintered units piecemeal. Fortunately Terry detected the ruse and wisely kept his men together. However, his march carried the troops deep into enemy-dominated terrain where he found himself threatened amid uncertainty. Terry hastily formed a hollow-square defensive position on the valley floor. It was a position from which the Indians, utilizing the hills nearby, could have besieged Terry's force at will.

Rather than pressing their advantage, the Indians, for their own reasons, chose to march the entire village mass of warriors and families away to the south. Seeing the Indians gone on the following morning, Terry formed and subsequently publicly proclaimed that corollary army "success theme"—that his movement south up the valley with his blocking-force troops had *compelled* the Indians to "retreat," to "flee," to "escape" him. Terry's conception of thus "driving off" the Indians and thereby "rescuing" the 7th Cavalry survivors was so inconsistent with the field realities and potential of this massive Indian force, relative to Terry's meager troop unit being fully vulnerable deep within the Indian war-zone, that only the deeply entrenched army attitudes of invincibility (against the Indian foe) can explain his entertaining such a mistaken view.

Neither Terry, his superiors, nor most of the campaign officers in their lifetimes understood that the Montana troop blocking-force, despite its susceptibility to being wiped out under siege, *had been spared by deliberate Indian choice.* That the Indians chose not to place Terry under siege and destroy his force was to their credit. It revealed, among other things, that from the beginning, Indian motives had been that of peaceful pursuits, roaming in their unceded lands, and not the killing of army troopers.

A variety of reporting inconsistencies and misconceptions are also found in the official records—notably the *1876 Secretary of War Report.* General Sheridan's personal report is included therein. Its tone and content are of particular interest, the following treatise providing extensive discussion on key points. Terry's personal reports are also embodied therein. The reports of both officers are so at odds with the facts of what actually occurred during the respective Custer and Terry troop marches of June 21-27, however, that one must question the motivation of these officers knowingly placing such inaccurate and misleading statements in the official records for all time.

Consider finally what is perhaps the most notable misconception. It can properly be termed *the personalization of the 1876 Little Big Horn campaign in Custer's name.* Recall how often book titles and other literary reference is made to the expedition being *his* campaign (Custer's Last Campaign, etc.), the countless books, articles, and films presenting the 1876 expedition as though Custer was the central, the dominant figure—as if all hinged on his presence, his leadership, his actions, virtually all other army participants thereby pushed to the background as of little significance, receding into historical obscurity by comparison.

It is unfortunate for history that such a major military adventure by the army in the development of the American West has been contorted into one man's personalized endeavor. This Custer-oriented author viewpoint arises in the literature despite the true facts so clearly evident in the records showing the exact opposite—e.g., Custer did not plan or command the expedition, or even lead the march west from Fort Lincoln; he was *a subordinate officer throughout,* in some disgrace at the time; he led only a portion of the troops involved, and was assigned a limited (though important) role in General Terry's *total plan* against the Indians who eventually cornered and killed Custer and his troopers.

Despite the color and drama of his tragic demise, Custer was *not* the central or dominant campaign figure. Precisely how such unwarranted and lofty status for Custer has distorted the official records and arisen in the subsequent public literature, and how such disproportionate attention to him personally, and to his specific troop actions has warped public understanding of the overall Little Big Horn campaign is discussed at length in **A Sad and Terrible Blunder.**

I sincerely hope the reader enjoys reexamining General Custer's final hours in this new factual light.

Roger Darling

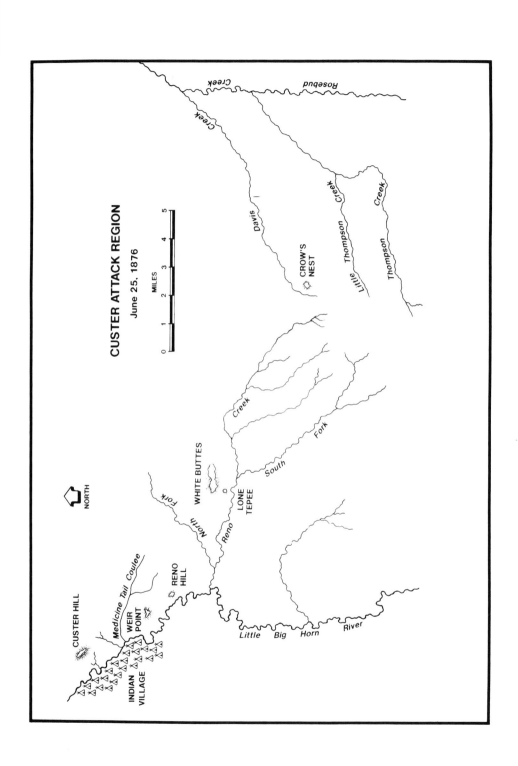

CUSTER ATTACK REGION

June 25, 1876

MILES

0 1 2 3 4 5

NORTH

Rosebud Creek

Creek

Creek

Davis

CROW'S
NEST

Little Thompson Creek

Thompson Creek

Creek

South Fork

Fork

WHITE BUTTES

LONE
TEPEE

Reno

North Fork

Fork

Medicine Tail Coulee

CUSTER HILL

WEIR
POINT

RENO
HILL

INDIAN
VILLAGE

Little Big Horn River

General Custer's Final Hours:
Correcting a Century of Misconceived History

In less than ten hours, General George A. Custer would be dead. Leading his entire 7th Cavalry, a twelve-company army regiment of over 600 men, on a sweat-drenching, dust-choking march up Davis Creek in the early morning hours, he now approached the ridge-divide between Rosebud Creek and the Little Big Horn River, Montana Territory. From the Crow's Nest promontory on that divide, Custer obtained new operational intelligence on the many Indian tribal bands he was pursuing. The day was June 25, 1876. [1]

It was minimal information indeed, hardly facts. Faint blue smoke and dust clouds hovering above the ground some 15 miles distant indicated Indian habitation and a probable, milling pony herd of great size. Custer's Crow scouts told him it was enemy presence in the elongated, north-south Little Big Horn valley. While viewing to the west, Custer commented on his long plains experience and excellent eyesight. However, even with army field-glasses better piercing the morning haze, he could not confirm, and did not credit fully what his Crow Indians, his "wolves" as they were called, reported. With this modest new data in hand he moved his troopers toward the distant valley. [2]

Custer's death, along with nearly half the 7th Cavalry about 5 p.m. later that day, would be viewed as dramatic, if not climactic American history. A century of tradition would be that the dashing Custer and his heroic cavalrymen were executing a clever, tactical pincer-maneuver against an Indian village, only to suffer defeat from overwhelming numbers of hostile savages. [3]

1

This tradition is not only inaccurate public press and history, but seriously flawed military assessment and analysis. Like many other commentaries on army unit actions carried out by General Alfred H. Terry, Colonel John Gibbon, Major Marcus Reno and Captain Frederick Benteen during that 1876 summer expedition against the Sioux, Cheyenne and other tribes, Custer's specific tactical performance between the divide and his death-ridge near the Little Big Horn River has been grossly misreported. The events have been miscast in countless books, magazine articles and film productions. The official government records have been instrumental in carrying forward the inaccurate information—e.g., the *1876 Secretary of War Report,* the 1879 Reno Court of Inquiry proceedings, and General Terry's 1876 field reports and letters.

The basic reason for such misconceived history is evident. Custer's contemporary officials and later writers have given him what might be termed a "free ride" on his operational intelligence. They have attributed to Custer specific terrain knowledge, Indian location information, and other field data they subsequently learned of in their own studies of his final hours, but which Custer did not and never could have possessed at given points or stations along that march route to his death-ridge. To overcome this error in Custer literature, both archival and precise field research on his last march route has been undertaken. The results are now available. They clearly define what operational intelligence Custer possessed (and did not possess) at several key locations.

History can be served by reviewing Custer's final actions in this clear, new light.

Even a limited examination of the operational intelligence elements associated with Custer's final movements, as permitted by this short treatise, clarifies the discrepancies between what might be termed the traditional history versions of Custer's demise, and what his field actions actually constituted in military terms that June day, 1876.

General Terry, the Expedition Commander, sent Custer and his 7th Cavalry up Rosebud Creek on June 22 to carry out half of Terry's cherished strategic plan against Indians suspected to be in the distant Little Big Horn valley region. Custer and his entire regiment comprised the attack-force in that plan; Terry, leading Colonel Gibbon's Montana troops, constituted the blocking-force.

Custer's business-like command, his methodical caution and prudent security measures were impressive from the march outset. The troops were tightly organized and disciplined. Custer considered his regiment under Indian surveillance at all times. Indian attack was to be expected at any moment, and in that event all had prearranged battle stations—e.g., stable guards, packers and cooks would protect the animals. No bugle calls, no noisy demonstrations or gunfire were permitted; men would sleep with their weapons. [4]

Lining the valley were multicolored sandstone buttes and crags, made even more beautiful by scattered pine growth. In all directions this rough terrain received Custer's rapt, patient attention. His short, punctuated marches and continuous efforts to keep the scout and cavalry units within supporting distance of each other belied later claims that Custer, once free of Terry's control, was bolting impetuously to find Indians for an early solo attack, glory for himself and beloved 7th Cavalry. [5]

Though naturally anxious to enhance his Indian fighting reputation, Custer was no such one-dimensional commander. This he demonstrated by various actions. At his crisp command, the entire column was halted for over four hours on June 24 at Great Bend near Greenleaf Creek. He felt the delay was necessary to allow scout chief Lt. Charles Varnum to backtrack and check a possible eastward deviation of the massive Indian trail, overlooked earlier. Custer's march up Davis Creek that night itself was prompted by positive tactical considerations. He told Lt. Edward Godfrey and other officers:

> "... he was anxious to get as near the divide as possible before daylight, where the command would be concealed during the day [June 25], and given ample time for the country to be studied, to locate the village, and to make plans for the attack on June 26th." [6]

This clearly expressed desire to honor Terry's strategic plan outline, and coordinated attack date with the blocking-force revealed Custer's sense of professional readiness and duty compliance. It was the frame of mind which distinguished his leadership and battlefield successes during the Civil War.

On that hazy morning of June 25, as he looked out from the Crow's Nest, whatever assumptions Custer entertained about his scouts' reports of Indians ahead, nothing obscured the operational intelligence facts plainly before him. The information was very limited. Most persuasive was the Indian trail which they had pursued for three days. Enormous in size and growing, it now swept over the high ridge-divide ground and disappeared down the winding Reno Creek to the west. Diverse track-markings testified to many Indian tribal bands coalescing in some form—perhaps in one or many villages strung along the vast Little Big Horn valley. Neither the Crow nor Ree (Arikara) scouts knew for sure.

One distinguishing trail feature pointed to the presence of Indian women and children, and a large pony herd in tow. Such Indian family presence held distinct advantages for the pursuing army troops. It limited their campsite selections and slowed the Indian march. It also constrained the natural flexibility of the warriors' attack-oriented, guerrilla warfare capacities. The only concrete intelligence indicating Indian habitation to the west, however, was a lone tepee standing beside another which had fallen—this seen by Lt. Varnum on a low plateau near some white buttes about half way to the Little Big Horn valley.[7]

As he was about to depart the Crow's Nest and to deploy his troops for the day of concealment, Custer was confronted suddenly with new intelligence. Lt. Tom Custer, his brother, and Crow Indian scouts reported three separate sightings of enemy Indians near Davis Creek. An Indian man and boy passed near the stream head. Seven Sioux appeared briefly on a hillside, and several Cheyenne were seen hacking open a cracker box that had dropped earlier from the regiment's mule pack-train.

Custer rode down to his troops and called an officers' conference. Those who attended never forgot his briefing: thus discovered, all hope of "surprise" was now lost, and to prevent the Indians from "fleeing," it was necessary to "attack at once."[8]

This critical moment was the origin of Custer's demise. It was also a point of departure. For reasons known only to him, there now began a fundamental transformation of Custer's behavior. While it should have been no surprise to him that Indians had seen the regiment, that fact alone appears to have loomed disproportionately, and became a catalyst of an unfortunate unraveling of his heretofore clear thinking as a dependable, subordinate commander approaching Indian warfare. Calculated restraint was thrown off. The calm composure of his leadership up the Rosebud was not only shredded now, but replaced with fitful haste, as if the scent of battle had eroded Custer's keen military judgment.

Traditional historical accounts in Custer literature convey the assumption that this "discovery" of the regiment automatically necessitated and justified immediate attack. Writers carrying forward this mistaken military assessment have found reinforcement by none other than the then Secretary of War and Civil War hero, General William T. Sherman.

Commenting in *The Army and Navy Journal* a month after Custer's death, Sherman expressed the view that according to the "rule" of Indian fighting, Custer ". . . could do nothing but attack when he found himself in the presence of Indians." [9] The remarks are revealing in several ways. By that date, Sherman and the army were embarrassed by Indian successes in nullifying that initial thrust of the 1876 expedition mounted so confidently against them. But beyond providing something approaching a generalized army excuse, or a specious doctrinal justification for Custer's failed "attack" actions, it indicated that senior army levels harbored gross misconceptions about the precise nature of plains Indian guerrilla warfare—an arena where very few "rules" applied. More importantly, Sherman's comments contradicted the operational intelligence facts that had been available to Custer, and on which he had based his "attack."

At the divide, Custer was not "in the presence of Indians" any more than he had been for days previously. The few isolated Indians suddenly seen were no threat to him. The vast, nebulous Indian grouping somewhere to his west, however, could be a threat, and these few Indian observers could be presumed to report west that they had seen him. But they might *not* do so, or perhaps take some time to do so. Any hasty "attack" actions would thus forfeit advantages to Custer in the event such an alarm was *not* given.

The time and distance factors were in Custer's favor. They alone precluded any need for abrupt decisions or undue haste. A march to the Little Big Horn valley was three or four hours at cavalry marching speed. This gave Custer ample opportunity to obtain data on the location of his primary enemies, and to make reasoned, strategic and tactical decisions for applying his force-structure against them. By contradicting these facts, and by endorsing Custer's haste, Sherman conveyed also a sense of blind army reaction—"could do nothing but"—offering no room for cautious judgment, or flexibly reevaluating sensible alternatives in the face of this modest Indian "discovery." In this regard, Sherman did not mention the most important element. Custer was not operating alone. He constituted *only half* of General Terry's strategic plan. Whatever Custer now did would affect the other half—the blocking-force.

With his own eyes, Custer had seen the labyrinth of coulees and rough, forested hills stretching miles west to the Little Big Horn valley. Unseen bands of camping Indians could be anywhere in that maze. The valley itself, an elongated fifty mile expanse, as yet gave no specific evidence of Indian habitation. The very concept of "attack" at this time was therefore incompatible with the operational facts then known. Attack what? No definite target or targets existed around which Custer could design his force-structure or tactics for an assault. It would be imprudent, and high-risk, to begin deploying troops before defining his target(s).

The attack concept was also inconsistent with that data pointing to a priority need for more information, and to maintaining troop cohesion coupled with marching caution until it was obtained. The information available justified only a reconnaissance march. This would be a less dramatic intermediate tactic than the action-oriented Custer may have preferred at the time, but one more operationally appropriate in view of the fact Custer was quite helpless at 15 miles distance to take any action precluding the Indians west from "fleeing." Persuasive in this regard was that trail data pointing to the presence of Indian families. It gave some assurance that thus encumbered, no Indians would be fleeing very far or very fast, whenever they got word that cavalry troops were nearby.

How did Custer utilize his operational intelligence at the divide?

Not persuaded by the inherent limitations of the available intelligence, he began deploying his troops as if he had a clearly defined target. At noon, the regiment crossed just west over the ridge-divide, and halted. During this short time since learning the regiment had been seen, Custer designed a strategy—a two-prong attack-thrust to the west. Two separate columns would make a rapid march toward the Little Big Horn valley, flushing and defeating any Indians met along the way.

During the halt, Custer selected Captain Benteen to lead the first prong of his "attack." With three companies comprising some 125 men, 25% of the total force, Benteen was dispatched southwest over an expanse of broken ground—coulees and rolling hills prevailing. This movement became known later as the Benteen Scout-to-the-Left. Curtly overriding Benteen's suggestion to "keep the regiment together," Custer ordered a dual mission for him—reconnaissance *and* attack. Benteen was to continue ever west from valley to ridge to valley to ridge, to report any Indian sightings, and, to ". . . pitch into anything" he came across. This dispatch of Benteen's force was the first, concrete, command-action evidence that a profound transition was taking place in Custer's military reasoning.

Custer, with seven companies of the regiment (67% of the force), would attack-march down Reno Creek. His troops comprised the second prong of his "attack." One company (8% of the force) was left with the pack-train, and ordered to follow on Custer's trail as rapidly as possible. Captain McDougall commanded the pack-train. [10]

By 12:30 p.m., both attacking units were moving west.

At best, good operational intelligence provides a commander reasonable certainty in applying military force to a specific target. Custer's westward attack-thrust from the divide, however, is characterized as a movement into near total uncertainty. It was high-risk. Custer assumed that he was dominant and in an offensive, operational mode. His comparative strength against his enemy was unknown, however, thus rendering his assumption invalid. This target intelligence-void placed him only in a defensive-probing mode, merely continuing his reconnaissance foray already carried out for three days up the Rosebud, seeking his enemy. Custer was *still* seeking his enemy. In realistic terms therefore, deploying Custer's and Benteen's troops comprised no attack on *any* enemy target(s). In this context, the military concept of "attack" existed only in Custer's thinking. At best, the respective movements of the two attack prongs constituted an "attack" *against a broad geographical region*, all in the confident expectation that an up to now illusive, if not phantom enemy would appear, be fought, and defeated.

Each attack prong was considered self-sufficient. The fact that the dispatch of Benteen's troops weakened Custer's main-force (as well as contributed to Benteen's vulnerability) did not alter concern over the uncertainties. Any risks associated with the sudden eruption of fighting were minimized by presumptions that in whatever numbers or configurations Indians materialized against *either* attack prong, each would prevail ("pitch into"—i.e., automatic success expected) in their respective spheres.

The need to communicate rapidly, particularly for such purposes as coming to each other's aid, was obviously not seriously considered in this context. But the terrain itself dictated otherwise. Notwithstanding, the nearly 80 square mile domain the troops were now entering, the uncertainties about the vast distance to cover over unfamiliar rough ground were lost amid Custer's confident expectation that Benteen would have no trouble reporting Indian sightings to him. In a similar disregard of unseen terrain obstacles, such as no passable trails over the ridges, and the possible absence of fords, Custer expected the two attack units could also regroup at his command.

The data-void suggested the wisdom of at least temporarily maintaining a compact force-structure and launching the Benteen scout farther down Reno Creek. By marching as a unit to a further point, the command would maintain greater strength, and might by then procure useful information on such matters as the ground surface near the Little Big Horn River, fords, and access to any target(s). Nothing would be lost by waiting to separate the forces. Custer disregarded and forfeited this operational advantage by dispatching Benteen from the divide. [11]

Forty-five minutes into the scout, Benteen's troops crossed a high ridge, and viewing north could see and hear Custer's troops on Reno Creek over a mile in the distance. The men were cheering and firing off their weapons, thus confirming that Custer was indeed pressing ahead with at least the cosmetic semblance of *an "attack" on the region* to his west. Lt. Godfrey later recalled the moment:

> ". . . During the march to the left, we could see occasionally the battalion under Custer, distinguished by the troop mounted on gray horses, marching at a rapid gait. Two or three times we heard loud cheering and also some few shots, but the occasion of these demonstrations is not known." [12]

In contrast with Custer's hushed march up the Rosebud, the boistrous march down Reno Creek revealed that Custer deliberately had chosen also to forfeit any advantages arising from the probability that those few Indians who had "discovered" the regiment at the divide, less than an hour before, might *not* forewarn the Indian assemblage to his west.

In this posture of relaxed marching caution, Custer covered eight miles and approached the lone tepee near the white bluffs, just north of Reno Creek at 2 p.m. [13]

A small village band of hostiles had occupied the site, probably camped for a few days enroute to join the main Indian group farther west. Alarmed at the enormous dust clouds and noise accompanying Custer's attack-march down the stream toward them, the Indians hastily packed and fled westward toward the Little Big Horn River. Custer's advance scouts had gotten so close they saw women abandoning cooking utensils on their fires and riding off on heavily laden ponies. A rear guard of some sixty warriors covered the retreat. Clearly unafraid, the warriors galloped just far enough ahead of the scouts to taunt them, inviting pursuit. [14]

Taking in the situation, Custer halted the command. Here was the first campaign fruitage—the first Indians flushed by his "attack" from the divide. They were not many in number, perhaps a hundred total, with some sixty warriors. From what Custer could observe personally and garner quickly from his scouts, the Indians manifested audacity and arrogance in showing no fear even of the now arriving troopers. Within minutes, Custer ordered Major Reno to take three companies (25% of the regiment force) and pursue this fleeing village band, to bring it to battle wherever it went. Concurrently, Reno was informed that Custer would support him "with the whole outfit." The orders were not written, but verbal, given to Reno by Custer's Adjutant, Lt. Cooke.

In describing this important moment in Custer's final hours, traditional accounts portray the following: Custer knew that a large Indian village was just beyond the bluffs to his northwest; Custer knew it was the only hostile Indian village nearby; and, Custer ordered Reno to attack that large village. All of these premises are untrue—misconceived history. Each premise is contradicted by various recorded historical facts: Custer's scouts provided no evidence of a large village at this time; Custer's orders to Reno made no mention of such a village; Reno recorded that he did not know of the village until he had marched nearly into its midst, much later.

Folk wisdom has it that if inaccurate statements are repeated often enough, they become history. Such error is a central problem in the saga of Custer's final hours, and here requires brief comment. The historical cost of accepting as true the above premises is to warp important campaign events not associated alone with Custer—e.g., to seriously alter the military significance of all subsequent campaign actions of General Terry, Captain Benteen and Major Reno. This is not the only cost. The events surrounding Custer *after* his departing the lone tepee area are *also* adversely affected in a way that dilutes understanding of Custer's field performance, his martial competence. By virtue of these false premises, Custer is given unwarranted credit for worthy motives and astute generalship and tactics in pursuing his "attack" from the divide to his death-ridge. In effect, these premises, by their peculiar nature and time of occurrence in his final hours of march, form the basis for focusing undue attention on Custer's campaign actions alone, giving them military significance the complete operational facts do not justify.

Officials and writers relying on these false premises never explain in their accounts how Custer, during his brief two hour ride from the divide to the lone tepee, acquired such operational intelligence telling him of *both the certain existence and location* of that vast single village. Invariably providing no source, they simply *presume* that Custer knew of the village, and then proceed with their narratives as if *in fact* he did know this. A century of such accounts repeating the same presumptions has cemented this false belief into the American consciousness as unquestioned history.

But as stated previously, this anomaly in Custer literature constitutes giving Custer a "free ride" on operational intelligence, attributing to him information he did not and never could have possessed. The lone tepee events provide an ideal example of the "free ride." Because writers later learned in their studies of the battle that there was a big village to the northwest, they assume that Custer also knew this at that time; because they later learned it was the only village, Custer also knew it was the only village; and, because (as will soon be seen) Reno eventually arrived at the south end of the village while pursuing an Indian band, Custer must have ordered him to attack that big village.

The absolute entrenchment of this historical inaccuracy is all the more remarkable in that the myriad of recorded facts about what Custer knew and did at the lone tepee, not only *do not sustain* these three false premises, but *indicate the exact opposite*. So tenacious has been the grip of these premises on Custer authors that none have probed deeply enough to question them at all, and thus never learn that Custer could not have, and indeed *had no such knowledge* of the vast village near which he later perished. In dealing with this "free ride" problem here at Custer's dispatch of Major Reno, the proof of such misconceived history is readily at hand.

The operational intelligence available to Custer at the lone tepee exceeded that which he possessed at the divide. He obtained some new terrain information from his own observations in riding to the tepee. It was of little significance. Other data came to him from his scout-intelligence force, at this time operating as two separate units: Lt. Varnum with the Ree Indian scouts; Mitch Bouyer leading the Crow scouts, including the young Curley.

Arriving at the lone tepee region about an hour before Custer, Lt. Varnum cautiously moved his Ree scouts south of Reno Creek and scanned the region from the protection of some low hills well back (east) of the Little Big Horn-Reno Creek junction. Also, an hour before Custer arrived, Mitch Bouyer with his Crows, and without detection, mounted the white bluffs and made observations from there, particularly noting the lone tepee village band's preparations for hasty departure. Both Varnum and Bouyer reported their operational intelligence findings to Custer *before* Reno was ordered in pursuit of the lone tepee band. What did the two intelligence units report to Custer at this time?

In his later writings, Lt. Varnum commented on his limited observations into the Little Big Horn valley, noting that the river east-bank bluffs obstructed clear views northward. Directly opposite Reno Creek mouth, however, a part of the valley floor was seen. A few isolated tepees were observed at the far western edge of the valley, indicating some minor evidence of enemy Indian habitation. But Varnum had *not* seen the vast village, the three mile long and one mile wide encampment which existed in a pocket behind the curving river bluffs. Line-of-sight field research observations from Varnum's viewing station(s) confirm the extent and limitations of what operational intelligence he could have reported to Custer on what existed in the valley. [15]

Mitch Bouyer perished with Custer, thus leaving no record of lone tepee events. Scout Curley survived, and later with notable consistency on a few critical points relevant to the lone tepee activities, provided historian Walter Camp with reliable accounts of the limited operational intelligence passed to Custer *before* Reno was ordered in pursuit of the lone tepee band.

Curley's basic report was simple. The Crows had watched the Sioux, the ". . . lone tepee in Indian camp was down under them to left. . . ." Using field-glasses and able to observe in all directions, (from the white bluff top) the Crows had primarily noted *only* the lone tepee village band immediately under their viewing station(s). A distant large Indian village was *not* mentioned in any manner by Curley, and the reference to the lone tepee band itself was modest. Curley told of its hasty departure, and Custer's soldiers setting fire to the standing tepee when they arrived. Line-of-sight field research observations from the Crows' white bluff viewing station(s) confirm their ability to observe the lone tepee band, *as well as their inability* (due to the river bluffs that had also plagued Varnum's viewing) to see the vast Indian village in that pocket behind the bluffs to the northwest. [16]

How did Custer utilize his new operational intelligence at the lone tepee station? What were Custer's specific orders to Reno?

To verify if the premise is true that Reno was to attack the large village, such orders must be evaluated in the context of information passed to Custer by his two separate scout units. Recall that Reno received his orders while the fleeing lone tepee Indians were some distance ahead riding rapidly down Reno Creek. Fortunately for history, several soldiers and regimental civilians stood very close to Custer and Lt. Cooke as the verbal orders were given to Reno. The words were overheard by these men, who at the 1879 Reno Court of Inquiry provided their recollections.

Lt. George Wallace stated he heard the orders as follows:

> "The Indians are about two miles and a half ahead. They are on the jump. Go forward as fast as you think proper and charge them wherever you find them, and I will support you."

The words "on the jump" and "wherever you find them" refer to moving Indians. Dr. H.R. Porter's testimony specified Reno was to pursue and attack ". . . the Indians just ahead" (obviously not a distant unseen village).

Sergeant Edward Davern's words were probably those which helped create a century of confusion over the term "village" meaning not the village band, but the *vast village*. He stated Reno's orders were:

> ". . . The Indian village is three miles ahead and moving, and the general directs that you take three companies and drive everything before you."

The terms "ahead" and "moving" specify the lone tepee village band, not a static massive "village" to the northwest. [17]

Sergeant John M. Ryan's evidence stated:

> "We saw a few abandoned lodges [tepees] with the fronts of them tied up. . . . At this point I understood that Custer gave

the command to Reno to overtake those Indians, and he would support him."

The term "overtake" identifies the close target, not a distant (unseen) stationary village. Scout Fred Girard also carried forward the concept of "overtake" when testifying the orders were:

> ". . . to take his command and try to overtake the Indians and bring them to battle while he himself would support him." [18]

Perhaps the ultimate proof of historical confusion regarding what took place at the lone tepee station of Custer's final hours is Reno himself. At the Reno Court, and in his later writings, he stated knowing of no such enormous village when receiving his orders. He learned of it later when charging Indians down the Little Big Horn valley. The southern end of the village suddenly loomed before him, alive with more warriors.

How did Reno understand his orders? He gave various accounts, but all are consistent. In his official report, his testimony at the Reno Court, and later as quoted by Lt. Godfrey, Reno said the following orders were given to him near the lone tepee:

> ". . . Lt. Cooke, Adjutant, came to me and said the village was only two miles above, and running away; to move forward at as rapid a gait as prudent, and to charge afterward, and that the whole outfit would support me." [19]

Reno is obviously referring to the *moving village band* just ahead on Reno Creek, and not the vast Indian encampment he saw later in the valley over five miles away.

Other Reno Court testimony fails similarly to attribute to Custer, or anyone else at the lone tepee, knowledge either of the vast village, or that Custer gave orders sending Reno to attack it. It is a fundamental operational intelligence fact that in both Reno's mind as well as in Custer's, neither was focusing on any "village" other than the band of sixty warriors with families fleeing down Reno Creek near its mouth, a mile or two ahead. The traditional scenario thus defies the intelligence facts.

(NOTE: It may be helpful to comment here that it appears one primary cause of a century of misconceiving Custer's final actions after departing the lone tepee stems from official reports and other documentary renderings, such as trooper diaries, misinterpreting and then misstating Reno's precise orders. All of the nuances of Custer ordering Reno to chase a small fleeing *village* band are carelessly, inadvertantly, or conveniently oversimplified and telescoped into a condensed description of Reno being sent to chase, and then charge, the vast "village." They are not the same "village." Word-substitution is the primary culprit. The term lone tepee village band in the orders, as used by Sergeant Davern, for example, is carelessly transformed into meaning the great village Reno found a long time later. The Reno Court of Inquiry records have numerous examples of this unfortunate transference of meaning, this misapplication of terms. It is remarkable to consider that the 1879 Reno Court officers, and the lawyers present (including Lt. Jesse M. Lee, for the Court, and Lyman D. Gilbert, who represented Reno) did not detect these aberrations and correct them at the time, thus making the Reno Court proceedings (as they should have been) a timely, 19th Century recognition of precisely what Custer's final movements constituted in military terms. Not having done so, it has led to a century of perpetuated misunderstanding as to precisely what Custer sent Reno to do, and what Custer himself did thereafter.)

The weakening of Custer's command judgment at the divide was now continuing. Caution was replaced with rash, ill-conceived troop deployments. The very first Indians seen and flushed were to be brought to battle. Custer now had what was lacking at the divide—a concrete, definable target, something firm on which to base a tactical movement. But the target was minor, fragmentary—a band of sixty warriors with some women and children. It represented no target worthy of deploying another 25% of his force just to bring it to battle *wherever it went*—particularly since he had *not yet located or even defined* the vast Indian enemy target(s) represented by that enormous trail pursued for four days.

Thus, at the lone tepee Custer possessed new operational intelligence, but it was insignificant relative to his main Indian target(s). This data-void was compounded by the fact that Benteen had not yet reported his findings of any village(s) strung along the Little Big Horn valley. This meant that Custer's left flank was a blind spot, Indians could sweep down from the south from any village groupings existing in that direction. Custer's right was similarly obscure. Having no more exact knowledge of Indian presence than the fleeing lone tepee band, Indians could sweep up from village groupings to the north. By concentrating on a target fragment, Custer was weakening his attack-force relative to the as yet unknown, Indian main-force strength.

These intelligence voids apparently did not trouble him. Feeling he could forego specific target and enemy strength data, Custer, as revealed through the wording of his orders, manifested confidence that Reno, like Benteen earlier, would be self-sufficient against *whatever enemy force he met*. Custer presumed that his own five company force would also be self-sustaining, not seriously weakened by the loss of Reno's three companies. This imminent battle-ready posture of confidence was not underwritten by relevant intelligence data.

As ordered, Reno now led off down the creek. Custer followed on the same trail shortly thereafter with his five companies. The two units did not long remain in sight of each other. Reno covered the nearly three miles to the river and crossed west. Custer stopped a mile and a half behind, taking the occasion to water the horses before proceeding. Less than 20 minutes later, Custer remounted his men. But now, instead of continuing on west down Reno Creek toward the ford where Reno crossed, Custer turned to the north, riding up a broad coulee leading to the high bluffs along the Little Big Horn River east bank. [20]

At this station in Custer's final hours, traditional historical accounts portray his turn north from Reno Creek as a well-considered, tactical maneuver—Custer mounting a flank pincer-attack on the large village northwest, *in conjunction with Reno's movement against that same target*. This unfounded belief is an extension of the basic assumption that both Reno and Custer were aware of the vast village. The questionableness of Custer's maneuver to the north derives from recognizing the limited data he possessed at this critical point, and what tactics he expected such a shallow base of information to sustain.

Dispatching Reno to pursue the lone tepee band wherever it went was a commitment to action somewhere ahead—possibly southward, perhaps due west, or maybe northward into the Little Big Horn valley. Custer did not know where Reno's "attack" would be consummated. In this context there was no assurance Reno might ever again maneuver close enough to Custer for coordinated action of any kind. Wherever finalized, however, it was obvious that other hostile Indians, wherever located nearby, would be aroused within minutes to furious responses. Reno would be fighting shortly. Time was thus an important factor, magnified even more so by the information that Custer did *not* possess and which bore heavily on the tactics now being undertaken.

He had no intelligence on target(s) south or north, only on the small lone tepee band. Custer had no knowledge of what the terrain to his north front along the river east bank would permit in the way of obstacles or opportunities to whatever "plan" he had in mind. For example, it was unclear if he could eventually ford the river farther north; that the bluffs would screen his movements; that the ravines up ahead were not full of warrior bands waiting in ambush; that there existed ahead *a target worth attacking.*

Custer's orders to Reno had included the idea of "supporting him with the whole outfit." In precisely what form such support would be made was never known. Custer never told anyone surviving what he had in mind. His decision to turn right from Reno Creek was certainly a commander's prerogative, but was of questionable merit after advising Reno he would support him. Taking an unknown north course *away from* Reno's trail, and consuming much valuable time along the way, diminished the true meaning of "support." Reno expected Custer would follow him directly in his rear, be immediately aware of any pursuit-turns he might make. The support Custer had in mind, however, was of a peculiar nature of his own formulation. Whatever it meant to him, in actuality, and under these fast-moving hostile circumstances, it constituted a daring, separate, or solo "attack" adventure that Custer must have reasoned would indirectly be of some benefit to the overall operations *wherever* Reno pursued his lone tepee village band. What could those benefits have been?

Traditional historical accounts provide what might be called a fourth premise at the lone tepee station. It is generally assumed in the literature that Custer knew Reno would automatically turn north and eventually attack ("charge") the large village. The premise is false. It is an unwitting literary assumption on Custer's behalf, almost constituting an historical bias to give Custer the benefit of any doubt. It is unwitting in the sense that writers making the assumption may not realize that in so doing it conveniently establishes a foundation on which to attribute (falsely) to Custer at this time, a thoughtful military tactic—that by knowing of Reno's turn Custer was enabled to hastily and *legitimately* devise a "flank" or "diversionary" attack on that large village. Custer's turn north in this context is presented as merely another available option

—that as commander, he quite properly and simply changed his option from following up Reno's rear, to turning north. There was no such legitimate option.

This tradition defies all the inconsistencies between Custer's actual orders to Reno, and Custer's own later actions. Since Custer was uncertain of the terrain, and *when* or *where* Reno would end up in his pursuit, *his turn northward is stripped naked of all such tactical legitimacy, shorn of valid motives as to working timefully and meaningfully in concert with Reno, and, rendering him timely or significant support.* The questionableness of Custer's tactical maneuver here is not only in leading Reno to expect "support" and then abruptly altering its form, but in *Custer becoming fully committed elsewhere, marching blindly into uncertainty.* Relative to the operational intelligence available to him, *Custer's turn north is readily identifiable as a pure gamble,* a suddenly conceived maneuver. It risked the success of the attack-force mission.

Custer was now alone amid uncertainty, rigidly confident he could strike a significant solo blow on some vague, undefined Indian presence ahead. The true circumstances now confronting him were not the product of any clever or insidious Indian strategy or operational skills. The Indians were in some disarray, hastily mobilizing ad hoc to overcome the lack of forewarning their own security measures should have but did not provide.

Beyond the questionableness of Custer turning north without assurance Reno would also move in that direction is the element of time. Custer's actions gave every appearance that the loss of thirty or forty minutes expended by galloping to the distant bluffs was of no consequence relative to any warrior groupings now being aroused nearby. Yet, with time so critical, forty minutes moving away from Reno would not be supportive in light of the Indians having certain advance warning of Reno's and Custer's movements, and Custer not even knowing the ground ahead—*where or how* he could strike any blow. Once again he had no defined target. The operational intelligence he now had was little, if any, improved over that minimal information possessed at the divide.

Also, as the commander, Custer could not disregard that such movement away from Reno further strained the already feeble communication links between the far-flung regimental units. Custer's turn north created the ultimate fragmentation of his attack-force. Every element was moving in different directions, without coordinated purpose or contact, so completely dispersed as to be irrecoverable within reasonable time limits.

The tactical implausibility of Custer's turn north is revealed even more clearly by considering the operational intelligence he did *not* possess at that time. If while Custer was marching north, Benteen had suddenly appeared with word of numerous villages to the south, Custer's tactic would be seen as foolish—moving away from a known enemy presence (south) toward an unknown presence (north). In like manner, had Reno in his pursuit actually turned left (south) toward such possible village(s) as Benteen might have thus detected, Custer would be seen as obviously maneuvering uncoordinated with Reno, acting solo against an unknown target (north) while Reno was confronting a known target in the opposite direction (south). Both scenarios reveal that Custer did not know what Indian threat existed to his south, and was deliberately ignoring this fact. In not hearing from Benteen as to conditions on his left flank, Custer chose to disregard as unimportant the intelligence mission objectives once held so vital, and on which he had based the Benteen scout-to-the-left only a few hours previously. In this context, Custer's command reasoning is seen as highly elastic, capable of gambling that the movement of his five companies north would be successful *despite* operational uncertainties to his south.

This march north led Custer to Weir Point, a high promontory overlooking the region. From there he made observations of the valley to the west. For the first time he saw the extent of his Indian enemy. Some lower bluffs limited the view slightly, but he clearly saw the enormity of the village. His bugler, John Martin, later confirmed this fact. Martin, a recent immigrant, related other elements of Custer's reactions to the village—(Martin being the only source of Custer's last known personal actions).[21]

He said that the village was quiet, with little movement. Martin believed that Custer was of the opinion the village had been "surprised" and was "sleeping." If Martin is to be believed, it means that the Indian encampment, stretching three miles long and a mile wide, gave little indication of Indian presence or activity in all of that expanse. Even allowing for Martin's limited education, his questionable choice of words beyond his native Italian, there is conveyed by him the remarkable concept that Custer felt he had caught such a village napping in the afternoon, it being about 3:30 p.m. Martin, in Reno Court and other testimony, even reinforced this view. He recalled that Custer looked down into the valley, removed and waved his hat, exclaiming words that, even though not recalled exactly, indicated Custer and his troopers were in a jubilant and dominant posture.

Custer waving his hat is a key feature of this important moment. It is so because Lt. DeRudio and others in Reno's command saw him do it. Having turned north down the valley in his pursuit of the tepee band, Reno came upon the large village, was confronted with a multitude of warriors, and was quickly driven by them into the river-woods just under the bluffs.

One of the great mysteries in Custer's final hours is whether Custer at this time actually saw Reno's troops from Weir Point. Martin does not say, but DeRudio's Reno Court testimony matches the timing of Custer's arrival there. Reno's troops were there to be seen, though perhaps somewhat obscure in the woods. If Custer saw Reno's men, he was aware of several important operational intelligence facts. He knew that Reno's pursuit of that lone tepee band had (by coincidence) led him to this juncture with the enormous village. In light of the village size, Custer was aware that *Reno was no threat to it;* that Reno was *not* now on any "attack." Reno had been abruptly pushed onto the defensive in the woods, and was confronted with more hostiles than his 120 man force could handle for very long. If, on the other hand, Custer did *not* see Reno's troops at all, it would not have surprised him, for having launched Reno to attack the lone tepee band, he knew Reno might now be chasing them anywhere in the valley.

Neither scenario is critical. Since they were not operating in coordination, it is not necessary to confirm where Reno was at the moment Custer looked into the valley and saw the vast village of perhaps more than 1900 lodges, home to thousands of Indians. The important intelligence factor was the significant new information here available to Custer. Warned repeatedly by his Indian scouts over the past four days that an unusually large Indian assemblage was before him, Custer now had at his disposal absolute proof of the fact. The reality could not be minimized.

It was apparent at Weir Point that Custer was in the presence of extraordinary circumstances. This was an unprecedented massing of Indians, nothing like it ever before witnessed in Indian war campaigns. But there was even another operational dimension to consider. Still not having heard from Benteen on the intelligence he sent him to find, it could well be that this village before him *did not constitute all of his Indian enemies*. Notwithstanding such a larger menace, every physical feature now before Custer in that valley formed the basis for caution, at least some pause for tactical reconsideration, reevaluation of his present movements and their legitimacy. The available data literally demanded this command requirement, particularly since Custer was aware that his tactical maneuvers from the divide were high-risk in the face of many uncertainties.

Such reevaluation would have told Custer that not even his five companies of troopers were a threat to that village, much less in addition to any other village(s) possibly nearby. Yet, Custer's obsession with "attack" had grown so strong between the divide and Weir Point, that even confronted with this incredible Indian force before him, the spell was not broken. Martin reported later that, almost without delay, Custer commenced giving orders to continue his "attack," now to be directed specifically against the village target in the valley before him.

Transfixed in Custer's mind was some strain of reasoning that clung tenaciously to the idea that the hostiles were basically cowardly; would flee rather than fight; and/or, would be awed by his military force, whatever its size or configuration. In some strange way Custer had obviously deluded himself into invincibility, not just for his five companies at this important moment, but *earlier* for Benteen's contingent (to "pitch into" anything), and Reno's as well (pursue them "wherever they go.") The intelligence evidence is unmistakable in revealing that a sense of absolute arrogance and omnipotence here pervaded Custer's thinking. However, here again the realities differed sharply from Custer's perceptions. The idea of his 250 man force attacking approximately 1900 lodges, housing thousands of warriors and families, spread three miles long and a mile wide, was not a rational military maneuver under the circumstances of Custer's relative force-structure and strength.[22]

Traditional historical accounts in Custer literature portray that at Weir Point *Custer had no choice but to press on against the village,* and that he made a well-reasoned, bold, courageous assault thereon. Such tradition is misconceived history. To press an attack under the circumstances, even considering the Indian warfare arrogance extant in the 1870s army, bordered on the reckless. Any attack would be a high-risk contest of numbers disproportionately arrayed.

Notwithstanding Sherman's later comments, which have helped

cement the false tradition of Custer having no choice ("could do nothing but" attack) at the divide, as well as now at the village site, Custer had no compelling reason to plunge headlong into such a target. He had no responsibility to attack regardless of the consequences. To the contrary, he had a greater duty to his campaign objectives, to his attack-force troopers being able to fulfill their strategic plan mission *in coordination with* the blocking-force under General Terry. To risk all in one great gamble against such adverse odds, not only held ominous consequences for the security of the (smaller) blocking-force, but was in itself not a plausible military command action.

The challenge at this time was to reason as a commander recruiting his strength to fight another day. The intelligence pointed to it; the physical circumstances dictated it. But Custer could not bring himself to recognize the advantages of pause, or even temporary regrouping. He did not understand, or have the capacity at this time to emulate what can be termed the Indian concept of *tactical humility*—of "giving way," temporarily restraining aggressive drives for larger, later tactical objectives. Few army commanders in the late 1800s appreciated the tactic of Indian warriors abruptly breaking off the fighting when battle fortunes changed and were seen as suddenly unfavorable to them. Almost invariably, the Indian maneuver was branded as "cowardice," thus revealing little army grasp of the conceptual underpinnings of plains Indian, guerrilla warfare. In employing tactical humility, many Indians survived to fight again, to capitalize on better advantages at a later time. To them, "giving way" was not cowardice, but tactical wisdom, an entrenched, inherited part of their warfare tradition. It was pragmatic; the results proved its value.

Sending Sergeant Kanipe back on the trail to hurry forward McDougall's pack-train, Custer now ordered his troops to descend into Cedar Coulee and then Medicine Tail Coulee, and from there to press west down its rough surface toward the village. It was here, at this moment, that the Custer Battle—the march from the divide to the Indian village—was lost. The decision at Weir Point to continue his "attack" meant it was now only a matter of time before the natural consequences of Custer's sequential mistakes from the divide took their toll. From this moment the respective actions of each of the four 7th Cavalry units can be described in a word—salvage. Each pursued a desperate scramble to save what it could from the high drama set in motion by Custer's flawed tactical thinking. The moment was tragic because it was a gross departure from all the fine martial capacities Custer embodied. Custer knew better.

Once in Medicine Tail Coulee, Custer took one last known action of tactical importance. Bugler John Martin was given a written message for Benteen, and sent on the back trail to find him. The note advised that Custer had discovered a big village, and Benteen was to hurry forward— and, to bring the pack-train. The content, timing, and context of this note to Benteen are significant in several ways, particularly in further revealing the rambling, elastic nature of Custer's thinking at Weir Point, and during that ten mintues before sending Martin.[23]

Now fully committed into unfamiliar terrain at the very edge of a vast hostile village, Custer abruptly considered the latest phase of his "attack" plan to be incomplete. He changed his mind in Medicine Tail Coulee. He had determined that Kanipe's message was insufficient. Now he wanted the pack-train *and* Benteen. Custer was confused about his earlier troop deployments. Benteen did *not* command the pack-train, and was probably nowhere near it in still carrying out Custer's earlier orders to scout-to-the-left. Having no idea where Benteen might be at this time, Custer somehow envisaged that Martin would easily find him on Custer's old trail, and Benteen would quickly gather up the pack-train and bring it to him. But here the far-reaching negative consequences of Custer's earlier (premature) dispatch of Benteen were realized.

Benteen had been ordered into unknown, unfavorable terrain, without communication or regrouping assurance, and on other missions *then* of great importance to Custer—to gather intelligence and to fight on his far left flank. Custer's message to Benteen now constituted *an unrealistic expectation*. He could place no timely reliance on his order being achieved within the void of information as to where Benteen was located relative to those earlier assignments given him. Whatever "plan" Custer now hastily envisaged in his change of mind, he had no rightful assurance Benteen could suddenly be available for meaningful integration into it.

This last known command by Custer is thus consistent with those issued earlier while moving from the divide. There was gross discrepancy between what Custer envisaged in his mind, and what the extant operational intelligence facts could sustain realistically in terms of troop actions and deployments.

No one lived to describe what Custer's troops experienced from the time Martin left them in Medicine Tail Coulee to their all being killed on Custer's death-ridge a few miles west, these events occurring approximately between 4 and 5:30 p.m. The distribution of over 250 bodies indicated that all of Custer's men were driven by the Indians to the death-ridge area in disarray, each group and trooper fighting desperately along the way. On a small knoll at the highest point on the long ridge, Custer and a group of officers and men, including his two brothers and a nephew, hastily created a defensive position behind a ring of slain horses. There, a "last stand" was made. Indians swarmed up the knoll from all directions.

From Weir Point to death-ridge, the terrain and Indian presence had combined to nullify Custer's firepower and tactics to salvage his command. It was this fighting between Weir Point and Custer's death-ridge that is popularly and traditionally referred to as the famous "Custer Battle."

Although the details of the "last stand" and "Custer Battle" are admittedly and justifiably colorful and dramatic, deeply rooted in western American history, it must nevertheless be respectfully stated that those heroic actions of both soldiers and Indians have been historically miscast. They alone *do not* constitute the true Custer Battle. The actions therein are not critical to understanding, and in fact deflect attention away from the *true reasons* for Custer's death and the destruction of his five companies. Those reasons are found elsewhere.

Precisely how the Indians maneuvered to corner and kill each soldier or group of soldiers is of no military significance because this traditional "battle" embodies no known tactical or strategic elements worthy of deep study. The "battle" represents merely the rapid denouement of Custer's "attack" plan from the divide, as well as General Terry's overall strategic plan. We know nothing about Custer's plan (or plans), his tactical thinking after departing Weir Point, if or why he separated his five companies, how he ordered them about, and at what point in his thinking he made the startling transition of one moment believing he was on the offensive and the next abruptly realizing he was on the defensive and in mortal peril. To speculate on these matters is of no military importance since Custer had already placed himself in a hopeless strategic situation and the eventual outcome was virtually foreordained. A century of literary and film preoccupation with, and immersion in, this "massacre" scene, has not added any meaning whatsoever to the famous 1876 campaign military actions, writers speculating endlessly over just what Custer and his men did in those final minutes, and how each man died.

The traditional "Custer Battle" is more than historically miscast. This study breaks with the emphasis and focus on that final hour, the last minutes of killing. In revealing the true reasons for Custer's demise, this treatise also *redefines* the Custer Battle. The facts related to Custer's maneuvers from the divide-Crow's Nest region clearly indicate that his "battle" actually started there—it did *not* start on that terrain between Weir Point and death-ridge. It started with Custer's "attack" strategy conceived at the divide. Custer was *not* defeated about 5:30 p.m. that day in a "last stand." *He had already defeated himself through poor generalship* by virtue of his errant reasoning and flawed tactical maneuvers unsustained by valid operational intelligence.

This will be an unpopular view, but it is historically accurate notwithstanding. Because the color and drama of his troops being killed off one by one, with no survivor to describe the "massacre" has been a popular historical event, writers have drifted into repeated and deadening conformity with the "battle's" traditional unwarranted importance. It is thus essential to present the true facts and correct the historical record.

Custer was defeated as a result of the cumulative effects of his misconceived "attack" strategy originated at the divide. All the way to death-ridge, each of Custer's subsequent command actions contributed its part: the unfounded expectation that he could hastily "attack" a geographical region rather than a defined enemy target; the premature dispatch of Benteen on his scout-to-the-left; the boisterous gallop of his troops to the lone tepee region, forfeiting his advantage of not yet being reported as discovered; his disregard of the need for concrete intelligence data on what enemy force actually existed to his west, somewhere in the Little Big Horn valley region; the further reduction of his command by sending Reno to attack a minor Indian band, this at a time when Custer was aware a mass of main-force Indians must be somewhere nearby; the turn northward from Reno Creek into wholly unknown ground and uncertain offensive possibilities; and finally, his flawed judgment at Weir Point on seeing the massive Indian village and not recognizing the obvious enemy strength, and his relatively weak potential against it.

Like one bad move of a chess game successively compounding and jeopardizing those moves that follow, each of Custer's actions negatively reinforced its predecessor into an integrated, self-reinforcing mosaic of blunders. It was this collective totality of command decisions that led to, and was the reason for, Custer's tragic end. The true Custer Battle was lost at Weir Point well before any shots were fired. Custer's judgment to continue advancing from there doomed his troops and guaranteed that his widely scattered remnants would have to fight for survival wherever the Indians cornered them.

It is useful at this point to provide one illustration of how the nation's top military officers viewed Custer's final hours, and how they presented their understanding in the official documents. General Philip Sheridan's Report, included in the *1876 Secretary of War Report,* well illustrates how the official records have contributed fundamentally to a century of public misunderstanding of what took place on June 25, 1876.

Referring to the events as a "misfortune," and "a disaster for poor Custer," Sheridan described the official army version of the famous final march:

> ". . . the Indians were not aware of the proximity of Custer until he arrived within about eight or nine miles of their village, and then their scouts who carried the intelligence back to the valley were so closely followed up by Custer that he arrived on the summit [Weir Point] of the divide overlooking the upper portion of the village almost as soon as the scouts reached it. As soon as the news was given, the Indians began to strike their lodges and get their women and children out of the way. . . . Custer seeing this, believed the village would escape him if he awaited the arrival of the four companies of his regiment still some miles in his rear. Only about 75 or 100 lodges or tepees could be seen from the summit or divide, and this probably deceived him as to the extent of the village. He therefore ordered Major Reno with three companies to cross the river and charge the village, while he with the remaining five companies would gallop down the east bank of the river, behind the bluff, and cut off the retreat of the Indians. . . ."[24]

It is remarkable, if not inexcusable as a senior army official, that Sheridan would not, by November 1876 when the *Secretary of War Report* was completed, have a sufficiently accurate understanding of the Custer Battle terrain to realize not only that his account was grossly incorrect, but as such, it would leave a completely distorted picture of the events on public records for all time. Many of the aberrations in his Report are immediately apparent from the facts presented earlier in this treatise. Some specific items, however, warrant comment.

His tone is notable. Reflecting the army arrogance of the time, Sheridan says the Indians "would escape him," and Custer would cut off their "retreat." No mention is made that Indian behavior gave no evidence of escaping, or retreating—and that in actuality *the warriors attacked Custer, Reno and Benteen* despite having no assurances at all that other army troops were not in the region nearby. Sheridan did not recognize or admit that Custer was *never* in a dominant posture; he assumed the Indians automatically to be subordinate (inferior) to army tactics and power.

No creditable evidence has been shown that the Indians who discovered Custer at the divide carried "the intelligence back to the valley"—i.e., forewarned the village. To say that such scouts warned the village "almost as soon as" Custer arrived at the Weir Point overlook above it, and this caused the Indians to "strike their lodges," contradicts (among other things) the evidence of Custer being jubilant over "surprising" the village, catching it napping in the mid-afternoon.

That Custer saw only 75 or 100 lodges from his vantage point is geographically impossible. Relative to the actual village size, the Weir Point overlook gives at least a 90% viewing exposure of the three mile long village site. This is what Custer saw. It is misleading to say Custer was "probably deceived . . . as to the extent of the village." Sheridan also contradicts himself on the village size and its implications relative to Custer's tactics. Although fully conscious the village embodied 1900 lodges (or more), he considered such a human mass residing therein as nimble enough to "escape" Custer's grasp.

Equally flawed was Sheridan's understanding of the terrain and the geographical relationship of key locations. The Little Big Horn River bluffs physically do *not* permit a gallop "down the east bank of the river, behind the bluff, and cut off the retreat of the Indians." This contradicts Custer's own knowledge of that terrain. Upon departing Weir Point he knew of the land surface obstacles along the river (bluffs right to the water's edge, etc.) and thus took a route (time-consuming) directly away (east) from the river via Cedar Coulee, and then into Medicine Tail Coulee.

The most revealing terrain and operational discrepancy is having Custer make personal observations of the village *before* dispatching Reno, and Sheridan presuming the orders included *Reno attacking the vast village,* and *in coordination with Custer.* This reflects Sheridan misunderstanding the sequence of the final-hours troop march and lone tepee events leading to Reno's mission, and Reno's specific orders relative to the lone tepee village band. Reno's orders were given *at* the lone tepee (where the vast village could not be seen), while Custer viewed the vast village *from* Weir Point where it is visible and Reno had long since been dispatched—two different terrain points, miles apart. Failing to even mention the lone tepee village band, and Reno's relationship to it, Sheridan conveniently ignores and thus transcends this geographical impossibility, thus contributing to the historical record one of the earliest versions of the false tradition—Custer knowing of the big village, and sending Reno to attack it.

Additional portions of Sheridan's Report (not presented here) contain other major deficiencies. But Sheridan is not alone in blame. The misinformation in his Report is equalled in General Terry's earlier reports and letters—data which to a degree had contributed to Sheridan's confusion. There was ample time, however, between June and November, for Sheridan, had he desired to do so, to remove the obvious discrepancies by ordering supplemental reports presenting an accurate and consistent account of Custer's final hours. This was never done. It is sufficient then to say that *both* Sheridan's and Terry's reports are tragic examples of official misconceived history.

A century of traditional military history may have it that Custer and his heroic cavalrymen were executing a clever tactical pincer-maneuver against an Indian village, only to be defeated by overwhelming numbers of savages. But such is misconceived history. The proof of this has been found in that rather dry, writer-neglected but nevertheless revealing arena of military field operational intelligence. Facts garnered therein at each of the four stations of Custer's final march tell a completely different story.

Custer's death can now be properly attributed to command failure—an intelligence failure. It was not that the information was flawed, or even lacking. The truth of the Custer disaster is that the commander deserves no credit for astute generalship. Gambling high-risk against the uncertainties, Custer consistently detached himself from the realities confronting him during his final hours. He destroyed his own attack-force, and his campaign mission, by employing strategy and tactics which his operational intelligence could not justify.

FOOTNOTES

1. The diverse troop locations, unit strengths, marching conditions and general facts concerning Custer's movements on June 25, 1876, are confirmed throughout Custer literature. Those seeking greater familiarity with the immense quantity of such detail associated with each tactical maneuver described in this treatise, are referred to: Lt. Edward Settle Godfrey, "Custer's Last Battle," *Century Magazine*, No. 43, January 1892, 358-87; Captain Frederick Benteen, *Narrative* (as published in W.A. Graham, *The Custer Myth*), 177-82; the researches of Walter Camp, *Custer in '76; The Reno Court of Inquiry (Chicago Times* account), Old Army Press, 1972; officer diaries; and, officer reports appended to the *Report of the Secretary of War, 1876, Vol. I, 44th Cong., 2nd Sess., Ex. Doc. 1, Part 2.*

2. Bradley, Lt. James H., "Lt. James H. Bradley's Journal of the Campaign Against the Hostile Sioux in 1876 Under the Command of General John Gibbon," *Contributions to the Historical Society of Montana*, Vol. II, 1896, 163-64.

3. This statement of tradition is a composite, derived from a plethora of literature on Custer's demise. Particularly notable are books by Van de Water, Whittaker, Dustin, Graham, Kuhlman, Monaghan, Stewart and contemporary authors. Numerous articles and films carry this traditional theme, as does the *1876 Secretary of War Report.* The latter document, for example, utilizes phrasing that commends the army troops who were inadvertently cut down while executing worthy tactics in the face of insurmountable Indian numbers.

4. Godfrey, *Century Magazine;* Benteen, *Narrative.*

5. This criticism or accusation is almost universally mentioned in Custer literature, often given added emphasis as an attitude and desire originating *before* Custer's last march began on June 22 at Rosebud Creek mouth where General Terry gave him his orders. The night before, Custer reportedly authored an anonymous article for national publication in which he castigated Major Marcus Reno for weak actions during Reno's scout a few days before into Indian territory. Custer implied that Reno had missed a fine opportunity to pursue the Indian trail he had found, and to make a "telling strike," missing the chance to "make a name for himself." It is grossly unfair to Custer and bad history to

translate this and related fragmentary data into the profound concept that Custer was so singular or narrow in motivation as to be just waiting to get free of General Terry so as to hastily locate the Indians, make an early attack for glory. Custer should not be condemned for harboring the idea of seeking battle success, or having such a thought imply that *this alone* was motivating him. More important is the balance of facts showing Custer's actual field performance *after* June 21 —diligently adhering to Terry's plan, and tracking the Indians with patient, professional care. See *New York Herald*, July 11, 1876; and Hughes, Colonel Robert P., "The Campaign Against the Sioux in 1876," *Journal of the Military Service Institution of the United States*, Vol. XVIII, No. LXXIX, January 1896, 28-41.

6. Godfrey, *Century Magazine*.

7. Custer's actions at the Crow's Nest and also just after receiving reports of the regiment being discovered by Indian hostiles, are notably covered in the writings of Lt. Charles Varnum, particularly the book, *I Varnum, The Autobiographical Reminiscences of Custer's Chief of Scouts*.

8. Godfrey, *Century Magazine*; Benteen, *Narrative*.

9. *The Army Navy Journal* (General Sherman's Articles), July 22, 1876.

10. Godfrey, *Century Magazine*; Benteen, *Narrative*; Reno testimony in *The Reno Court of Inquiry (Chicago Times* account). The refinement of Benteen's orders to "sweep everything before him," is also found in the *Secretary of War Report, 1876*, 476, as well as in Reno's testimony.

11. The Benteen Scout is a notable void in Custer literature. All authors mention it in general terms but have not undertaken the field research to determine Benteen's precise terrain movements. The many elements entering into Custer's rationale for the scout, along with recent field research defining the march route and its timing, are found in the author's work: *Benteen's Scout-to-the-Left: The Route From the Divide to the Morass*, 1987. Custer had valid reasons for considering this scout action. At his 1868 Battle of the Washita (river), Custer nearly met with disaster by failing to pre-scout for Indian villages nearby the main encampment he eventually attacked and occupied. The unscouted villages were quickly aroused and organized to trap Custer for a time in the conquered village. Obviously benefiting from the sharp experience, Custer now wanted Benteen to determine if multiple villages were similarly strung along the distant Little Big Horn valley. This reason alone, however, was *not* justification to send Benteen on that mission *from* the divide. The same purpose would have been achieved sending Benteen from a closer point.

12. Godfrey, *Century Magazine*.

13. Lt. George D. Wallace, marching with Custer, carefully recorded the troop itinerary that day. (See *Report of the Secretary of War, 1877, Vol. II, Part II*, (Report of Lt. George D. Wallace, Seventh Cavalry).

14. *Reno Court of Inquiry (Chicago Times* account).

15. See Lt. Varnum testimony at the Reno Court, and also his statements in *I Varnum*. Lt. Varnum viewed from several points along the southern banks and hills near Reno Creek. The field research to determine what his observations could see from those points included compass transit sightings in all directions,

corresponding to detailed U.S. Geological Survey maps of the region. The Little Big Horn River east bank bluffs are notable in preventing (from all of Varnum's viewing stations) *any* sighting of that terrain covered by the vast Indian village.

16. Camp, Walter, *Custer in '76*, 156, 161. Also see Footnote 15 remarks on field research observations. Similar sightings were made from the top of the white bluffs, thus confirming that the Little Big Horn River east bank bluffs also obscured for the Crow scouts any view of that terrain covered by the Indian village.

17. *Reno Court of Inquiry,* 65, 188, 279.

18. *Montana Tribune,* June 22, 1923 (Sergeant Ryan interview); Graham, *Custer Myth,* (Scout Fred Girard quoted from the *Arikara Narrative),* 251.

19. *Reno Court of Inquiry,* 401.

20. The location where Custer turned north, and his trail thereafter, were studied by General Terry and his officers promptly after the battle. The location of the turn is not generally in dispute (North Fork junction with Reno Creek), although subsequent horse travel on Custer's trail north leaves some minor doubt as to his exact path. See *1876 Secretary of War Report* (General Terry's Report), 461-471.

21. Testimony of John Martin in the *Reno Court of Inquiry.* Also see various public statements made by Martin in Graham, *Custer Myth,* 121-322.

22. A notable feature of traditional Custer literature is the failure to take realistic note of the actual geographical size of the vast Indian village. At three miles long and one mile wide the encampment represented an enormous expanse. To aid students of the battle gain an accurate appreciation of that village size, so as to maintain balanced judgment relative to the tactical merits of Custer's 250 man force "attacking" it (or Reno's 120 man force later criticized for not "riding through" it rather than retreating into the river-woods), the author has often utilized a simple field exercise. It is suggested that a driver watch the terrain passing his car a half mile on each side of a straight country road while moving directly ahead at 5 to 8 miles per hour (approximate cavalry attack speed), going three miles and noting during the travel: how long it takes to drive the three miles; how many Indians and tepees would reside within that land surface; and, considering how in the face of such an aroused, ferocious populace 250 men riding openly on horseback (dodging among the tepees) could successfully deal with such a fluid enemy. The exercise invariably establishes better perspective on the physical circumstances of Custer's "attack" realities. The words extraordinary and unprecedented are seen to apply readily.

23. *Reno Court of Inquiry.*

24. *1876 Secretary of War Report* (General Sheridan's Report), 443-44.

BOOK AVAILABILITY

A Sad And Terrible Blunder, Generals Terry and Custer at the Little Big Horn: New Discoveries
by Roger Darling

- A comprehensive presentation of the *total* Little Big Horn campaign, *including* the most profound examination ever made of Custer's final hours.

- Winner of the 1990 John M. Carroll Literary Award.

(Hard cover, bound in Roxite Green, gold stamping, 315 pages (8½×11), 65 photographs, 18 maps, 21 "Photo Outline" diagrams, Foreword, 15 Chapters, Footnotes (annotated), Bibliography, Index)

Order from:

Custer Battlefield Historical & Museum Association (CBHMA)
P.O. Box 129
Crow Agency, Montana 59022

Phone: (406) 638-2382

($28.50 plus $5.00 shipping/handling = $33.50)

OR

Potomac-Western Press, Inc.
P.O. Box 1332-V
Vienna, Virginia 22183

($28.50 plus $3.50 postage/packaging = $32.00)

Books signed by author on request

(Potomac-Western Press makes no sales in California.)